I0460098

Wandering Woman: Arkansas

The Ultimate Road Trip: One Woman's Journey Across the United States by RV

Julie Bettendorf

Copyright © 2025 by Julie Bettendorf

All rights reserved.

No portion of this book may be reproduced in any form without written permission from the publisher or author, except as permitted by U.S. copyright law.

Contents

Introduction

"Not all who wander are lost." JRR Tolkien

Are you sure? I thought to myself, as I tried not to panic. I was a long way from anything familiar, but that was how it should be. I had driven thousands of miles on dusty, pothole-filled roads. It's often on the worst roads that you can discover something truly amazing.

My dusty CRV was parked beside me, containing one restless dog and a variety of snack bags, all empty by now. There were no buildings in sight, no cars or people or movement at all. Only the constant humming of the insects as they buzzed around my head.

I turned to my left – another straight road that trailed off into the distance. I glanced over to the right, then behind me – two more barely discernible roads stretched out into the abyss. I was in a four-way intersection with no signs, no sense of direction, and no sign of life for several miles. No cell service either. *Damn*, I thought. *I'm lost.*

How did I get here? I couldn't help but feel like this little intersection was a cruel metaphor for life. I began to daydream, imagining each road might transport me back to a different time, a different role in my life, and a different me.

If I took the road from whence I came, it could lead me all the way back to Oregon, back to my cheating third husband, back to a life of loneliness and solitude. There is no greater loneliness than being married to someone who isn't actually present in your life.

If I took the road to my left, perhaps it could take me back to my career as a dental hygienist, a job I hated deep down in my soul. There is something so disengaging about cleaning teeth for a living. It's a disgusting, smelly way to get a paycheck. It pays well, which is great, but the best part is the huge gob of friends I enjoy to this day.

Or maybe the road to my right, *yes – maybe that's the path*, I imagined. Maybe it could take me back to my real treasure, my kids. Back to their smiling, innocent faces as toddlers, as they danced around the Christmas tree and their father and I were still married. Back when they still needed me for every little thing.

But, that was just it. I didn't feel needed anymore. My kids weren't toddlers anymore – they were both full-grown adults, and far too busy for me. My dental buddies were still working, but I wasn't. Dental hygiene had robbed me of the cartilage in my fingers, giving me severe, disabling arthritis. And, I wouldn't be returning to any more husbands either, because three marriages were quite enough for me.

All three of these paths, all three of these roles – the wife, the mother, and the dental hygienist – had seemingly been stripped from me within a year. I was lost and looking to find myself again.

The funny thing about this phrase, "not all who wander are lost" – is that, in my experience, wandering and being lost walk hand-in-hand with one another, and the expression can be flipped. In my experience, not all who are lost are wandering, and that is a real disservice to the beauty and clarity that the world has to offer.

When one becomes lost, wandering is the only option to guide oneself back to a path. After all, one could not come upon any dirt path at all without wandering.

I began wandering at an early age, both with my mind and with my feet. At eight years old, I was reading a book about archaeology and dreaming of one day seeing Egypt. I didn't follow a traditional path in high school either, going heavily into foreign languages, in hopes of one day using them.

At twenty-five years old, I divorced my first husband (the dental student who talked me into becoming a dental hygienist so I could work for him) and decided to give traveling a real shot. I took off for the Andes and Macchu Picchu, climbing up ancient Inca stone steps to reach the magnificent ruins.

Anyone who has been to Macchu Picchu will tell you there is something ethereal and deeply spiritual about the place. The ruins stretch out across the emerald green mountains, way up in the middle of the sky. Macchu Picchu gave me my first experience of feeling history. This trip inspired me to come back and complete a degree in archaeology, and I've been wandering ever since.

More travel followed including a backpack trip around Europe for three months, by myself, and trips to Britain, Italy, and Greece. I visited the burial places of Crusaders, mummies, and ancient kings. I happened upon the castle of my namesake in Bettendorf, Luxembourg, and wandered my way through European history.

My favorite excursion by far was finally seeing Egypt with my daughter in 2012. Just like my childhood dream envisioned, I rode a camel beneath the pyramids of Giza, with my head wrapped in some man's sweaty turban. It was perfect.

Traveling has always been my own personal antidote to pain. I went to Mexico after my first and second divorces, Canada after my third, and Italy after my dad died. Call it avoidance if you want, but I call it an accelerated form of healing in the purest sense of the word. I believe travel can heal your soul.

Wandering has always worked its wonders on me – made me feel renewed, rejoiceful, grateful, and purposeful. It's been my medicine.

So, as I stood in that intersection, I once again wondered how wandering had led me so astray this time. *What the hell am I supposed to do now?* It was then that I realized that one last path had not been considered yet – the path which stretched straight out in front of me. *Which role does this represent?* I pondered.

The answer smacked me in the face.

That last dirt road – the only path that could take me where I wanted to go, the only path that ever truly healed me or showed me the way – was the path of the traveler. The wife, the mother, and the hygienist roles – though valued in their time – were sitting in the bleachers now. It was time to welcome and enable my boldest, bravest, and perhaps most pivotal role yet:

The role of the Wandering Woman.

Welcome to Wandering Woman

This book is for you – the grieving empty nester mom, the begrudged housewife, the woman in need of a drastic change in her life. Really, this book is for anyone with a passion for traveling. If you feel lost with no sense of direction or purpose in life, that's a bonus – this book will be even more appealing to you. And lastly, if you're a man reading this book, congratulations for holding a book with the word woman in the title. You're contributing to gender equality, and that's pretty neat.

I decided to combine three of my dearest loves – travel, history, and archaeology – and put them into a book because I believe wandering has the power to change your life. I have been to many areas of the world and have enjoyed too many outstanding experiences to list. However, by the time both my children moved out in 2017, I realized I was a stranger in my own country. It was the perfect time to explore a new country (my own) and discover a new me at the same time. I have been traveling for five years now, and I've upgraded to a small RV. I also have a new traveling companion, another sweet Sheltie, named Rosie. ***Wandering Woman*** is the chronicle of my journey across the United States, discovering the joy of getting lost and finding myself along the way.

Why You Need to Take a Road Trip

*A**merica, the beautiful?*** I sure think so, but I didn't realize just how beautiful our country is until I embarked on traveling across the United States, full time, in a small RV.

The United States offers something for everyone. From spectacular beaches, austere mountains, to rolling plains, our country has it all. It's difficult to comprehend just how large and impressive our scenery is, until you experience it first-hand, with the ultimate road trip.

I also realized just how much of our history is missing from U.S. history I was taught as a kid. The history of our country didn't begin with the pilgrims landing on Plymouth Rock in the 1600s. Our history is far more ancient, with rock art and archaeological sites dating back over 12,000 years.

We owe a tremendous debt to early pioneers who tamed our land. The Mormons and other groups ventured into the great unknown with their families and their worldly possessions. Some of them pulled cumbersome handcarts across the country to settle in inhospitable, dangerous locations.

The goal of **Wandering Woman** is to bring history back to life and make it interesting again. I am presenting some famous sites, and many little-known ones. You will take the road-less-traveled with me, while we explore ghost towns, rock art sites, archaeological sites, and museums, to discover the colorful tapestry that is our country.

I present some history, including dates, but my goal is to present more of the real-life stories of history, including ghost stories, profiles in history, voices from the past, and moments in time, to give you, the reader, a deeper understanding of the context of history.

This is by no means an exhaustive list of places to visit. In fact, I encourage you to discover America for yourself, as I am doing, by making a trek across the land by car or RV. You can venture forth as the early explorers did, just a little more comfortably, with a lot less hardship.

I hope you enjoy this book and take a little time out to discover our beautiful country, and maybe even discover yourself in the process.

Safe Travels,

Julie Bettendorf

Welcome to Arkansas

The Natural State

I love **Arkansas**. It's a state with so much history, and so many friendly, warm people. Arkansas is a place I can go back to many times, and still not see everything. It's called the "Natural State" for good reasons. The land is spectacular and unspoiled.

Five Things to Love about Arkansas:

- Amazing historic towns like Washington

- Unique, early history of the United States from places like Arkansas Post

- Mound builder archaeological sites like Plum Bayou

- Civil War history from places like Prairie Grove and Pea Ridge

- The many gorgeous campgrounds like Cane Creek

Dreams of Arkansas

"I was the fattest baby in Clark County, Arkansas. They put me in the newspaper. It was like a prize turnip." **Billy Bob Thornton**

"My family didn't have money to travel, so reading was how I knew about the world. It made me hungry to have more experiences than just what I could possibly experience in Arkansas." **Mary Steenburgen**

"If I could rest anywhere, it would be in Arkansas, where the men are the real half-horse, half-alligator breed such as grows nowhere else on the face of the earth." **Davy Crockett**

Famous People from Arkansas

James Black (1800–1872), manufacturer of the Bowie knife

Johnny Cash (1932–2003), country singer-songwriter

Bill Clinton (born 1946), 42nd president of the United States

Bill Doolin (1858–1896), outlaw and founder of the Wild Bunch, born in Johnson County

John Grisham (born 1955), novelist

Douglas MacArthur (1880–1964), US General of the Army, Medal of Honor recipient

Mary Steenburgen (born 1953), Oscar-winning actress

Billy Bob Thornton (born 1955), actor, Oscar-winning screenwriter

Sam Walton (1918–1992), founder of Wal-Mart Inc.

Early Arkansas

Early Arkansas Doctor

Pearl Harvesting on the Black River

Early Residents of Rush

Pea Ridge National Military Park

The *Pea Ridge National Military Park* is the site of a Civil War battle to keep Missouri part of the United States. On March 7-8, 1862, Union Army commanders, Brigadier General Samuel Curtis, and Brigadier General Franz Sigel faced Confederate Generals Albert Pike, Earl Van Dorn, Sterling Price, and Ben McCullough in combat at Pea Ridge. The Union Army was victorious, maintaining control of the area. The Confederate Army retreated to Fort Smith.

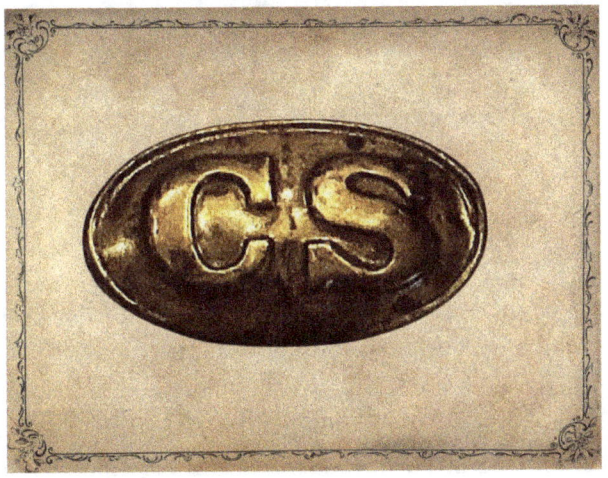

The Pea Ridge site has a fine museum with many artifacts from the war, including this belt buckle from a soldier in the Confederate Army.

One trail of the battlefield leads to Leetown, a small hamlet of houses which were used as hospital facilities for both the Union and Confederate armies. Yellow flags guided stretcher bearers to the site. As you drive the Battlefield tour, there are sites marking the locations of Curtis's headquarters, and the Trail of Tears, the route Cherokee and other tribes had to take when they were displaced from their homelands. There are also memorials to soldiers who died in the battle.

You will also see the lovely Elkhorn Tavern, originally built in 1833, and an official stop for the Overland Stage. By 1862, it became a Union Supply depot, and then was used by both Union and Confederate armies as a field hospital. During the battle, the upper level of the building was hit with cannonball fire.

The tavern gets its name from a pair of elk antlers attached to the roof. Confederates burned the original Elkhorn Tavern in 1863. What you see today is a wonderful reconstruction, built by Joseph Cox, shortly after the building burned. The southern chimney is original.

How to get to the Pea Ridge National Military Park:

The Pea Ridge National Military Park is located at 15930 Hwy. 62 in Garfield, Arkansas.

Voices from the past:

"Entering a little clearing, we discovered the yellow hospital flags fluttering from the gables of every house in the hamlet of Leetown, and the surgeons busy with the sad, yet humane task that was theirs to perform." **Lyman G. Bennett, private, 36th Illinois Infantry Regiment.**

Ghost Story:

Pea Ridge National Military Park was the site of tremendous violence, and it is known to have several ghosts. The Elkhorn Tavern was the site of some of the worst violence and suffering. Combat and the fact that it functioned as a hospital, make it a prime spot for paranormal activity. There are numerous reports of people sighting apparitions of Confederate soldiers,

A woman who lived near the battlefield as a child told of exploring she used to do, and of a chance encounter with ghosts. She and her brother were walking around the Elkhorn Tavern when they both spotted a group of Union soldiers in their blue uniforms and their horses tied up near the building. Suddenly the men mounted their horses, rode out, and disappeared. Others have experienced sounds coming from inside the tavern, as if someone is walking around. Other areas of the battlefield are home to the ghosts of Confederate soldiers and their horses. Moans, cries, and hushed talking have all been heard at Pea Ridge Battlefield.

A word about the Trail of Tears:

The ***Trail of Tears*** is one of the most shameful events in the relationship between Native American tribes and the U.S. government. It happened as a result of the Indian Removal Act of 1830. The Trail of Tears refers to the forced removal and relocation of thousands of Native Americans. Tribes impacted included the Cherokee, Choctaw, Chickasaw, Moscogee, and Seminole. These tribes were removed from their native homelands in Tennessee, Alabama, North Carolina, and Georgia and forced to walk west, eventually reaching Oklahoma. Over 10,000 Native Americans died on the 1200-mile journey, facing starvation and disease.

The Shiloh Museum

The ***Shiloh Museum*** provides a fascinating look at the life and history of people of the Ozark Mountains.

Inside the wonderful museum there are original walls from a log home built in 1841.

You will also enjoy a display of artifacts and history of medicine in the Ozarks. Plants and other natural ingredients were frequently used to treat illnesses. Doctors traveled on horseback to treat the sick, and they were often paid with barter such as eggs, corn, and ham.

"Granny women" and midwives performed important medical ser-
vices for their neighbors.

My favorite artifact in the museum is a shoe, once belonging to Sterling Price Graham, most likely named for Confederate General Sterling Price. Young Graham lived from 1862 to 1865.

Outside, you can also enjoy several historic buildings on the grounds, including the Steele General Store, built in the 1870s, Dr. Carter's Medical Office, built in the 1880s, the Ritter-McDonald Log Cabin, built in the 1850s, and the Searcy House, built in the 1870s.

How to get to the Shiloh Museum:

The Shiloh Museum is located at 118 W Johnson Ave. in Springdale, Arkansas.

Prairie Grove

The ***Prairie Grove Battlefield State Park*** **is** one of America's most intact Civil War Battlefields. On December 7, 1862, the Confederate army under Major General Thomas Hindman and Union armies under Brigadier Generals Francis Herron and James Blunt converged. Prairie Grove was the last major Civil War battle in Northwestern Arkansas, resulting in 2700 casualties.

Suffering continued after the end of the war, with the population of Washington County being reduced from 15,600 in 1860, to 5,800 in 1865. One Kansas soldier remembered seeing a Southern woman finding her dead husband's and brother's bodies a short distance from each other. Burial of all the dead soldiers took over a week.

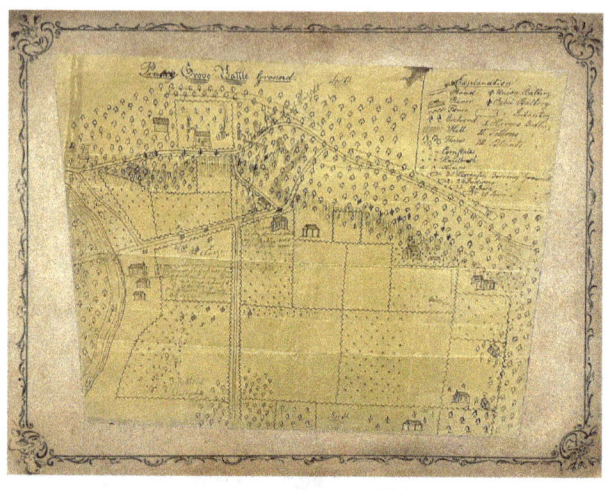

Prairie Grove has an outstanding museum in the Morrow House. The Morrow House was once the shelter for General Sterling Price and Earl Van Dorn as they prepared for the Battle of Pea Ridge. General Hindman used the house before the Battle of Prairie Grove. One of my favorite artifacts is a map of the battlefield, drawn by David Arthur of the 20th Wisconsin Infantry. The 20th Wisconsin lost 49% of its men in the first fifteen minutes of the battle.

As you walk around the battlefield, you will see the Borden House, built in 1868 by Archibald Borden, after his first house was destroyed during the battle. The heaviest fighting took place near the Borden House and orchard, where 250 soldiers lost their lives.

The Latta House, built by John Latta in 1834, is a two story log cabin. It was originally located twelve miles southwest of its current site. The upper floor has two bedrooms, and a kitchen in the basement. John Latta also had a barn and springhouse.

Don't miss the lovely schoolhouse, a small, sturdy log structure. The schoolhouse was used as a headquarters, and then a field hospital.

The current schoolhouse is a reconstruction. Materials from the original schoolhouse were used to make coffins.

How to get to Prairie Grove:

The Prairie Grove Battlefield State Park is located at 506 East Douglas Street, in Prairie Grove, Arkansas.

Voices from the past:

"The guns which had been belching flame and smoke all morning stood there still and cold, and the horses as if waiting for us. We could have taken the horses away, but some officer called out to shoot the horses. Men and officers called out in reply 'Save the horses.' Again the senseless order was repeated and this time obeyed. The beautiful horses were piled in a bloody heap." **20th Wisconsin Infantry officer, 1862.**

Ghost Story:

The Borden House was one of the most active battle sites in Prairie Grove. There are reports of people hearing footsteps and voices, as if someone is walking up behind you.

Another spirit haunting Prairie Grove is that of a little girl, who has been seen looking out the window of the Borden House and the Latta House, when both buildings are locked. The apparition fades away when people move closer. The sounds of a little girl laughing and giggling have also been heard. The spectre of an elderly man, who could be John Latta, has also been seen at the Latta House.

Fort Smith

T he original log and stone *Fort Smith* was built in 1817 and only the stone foundation is still standing. The fort was rebuilt of stone and brick, beginning in 1838.

It served as an important supply port during the US-Mexican war of 1846-1848, the California Gold Rush of 1849, and the Civil War, between the years of 1861 to 1865.

The Fort Smith Visitor Center is housed in the upper floor of the old jail. This jail was known as the Hell-on-the-Border Jail. The original jail had two large cells, each holding 50 men, with no sanitation other than a bucket in the fireplace. The jail had no heat, no air conditioning, and was filthy. Conditions were so awful that a new jail was constructed in 1888.

The same building also houses the courtroom of Judge Isaac Parker. He opposed the death penalty, but unfortunately still had to
sentence 160 men to death, 79 of which were hung at the gallows
nearby. Don't miss the ornate desk and chair belonging to Judge
Parker.

The first execution in the gallows happened in 1873. Although the gallows could accommodate executing up to 12 men at a time, the most men hung at any one time was 6. A total of 89 men were hung in 39 separate executions.

The Commissary building was built between 1838 and 1846, making it the oldest Fort Smith building still standing.

The Commissary building also contains cozy living quarters for the Hammersley Family, who helped Judge Parker in his duties.

How to get to Fort Smith National Historic Site:

Fort Smith National Historic Site is located at 301 Parker Ave, in Fort Smith, Arkansas.

Voices from the past:

*"The carpet bag (George) Johnson carried gave him dead away. In it was found several quarts of red liquor, a dice box containing six dice, (three of which were loaded) two packs of cards, a sweat cloth, and a lot of gaming chips. George was prepared to meet the boys on any ground. If he could not sell them the liquor, he could give it to them, and then win their small change after getting them drunk." **From the Fort Smith Elevator, December 7, 1883. Johnson pled guilty to introducing liquor into Indian Territory and was fined $50 and sentenced to one year in prison.***

Historic Washington State Park

*H*istoric *Washington State Park* is a lovely little town composed of the largest collection of 19th century buildings in Arkansas. In 1819, settlers and travelers stopped in Washington, while making their way on the Southwest Trail. James Bowie, Sam Houston, and Davy Crockett all visited Washington.

The town was named for George Washington, the first president of the United States. Washington was also the Confederate capital of Arkansas from 1863 to 1865. The Bowie knife was made here by James Black, the local blacksmith.

The Courthouse, built in 1836, dominates the town. The building was used when Washington was the Confederate capital.

The museum contains some wonderful artifacts uncovered during archaeological excavations. One of my favorites is a saucer which dates from 1822 to 1835.

The Crouch House, built in 1856, is one of the first historic residences you will come across as you walk the town.

It's a lovely residence, and one of many residences you can walk through on a tour.

The Royston House was built in 1845 for lawyer Grandison Royston, a member of the Confederate house of representatives.

On the grounds of the Royston House, you can find this lovely hitching post styled in a dog's head.

The Royston Log House, built in 1835, is a rustic, charming structure built for Grandison Royston, a prominent lawyer.

The interior of the home is sparse, but still appears comfortable and inviting.

You can also visit the print museum and weapons museums.

Don't miss the Pioneer Cemetery, containing several generations of Washington's first citizens. Burials began in 1825 and were discontinued in 1922.

The Block-Catts House, built in 1832, is close to the cemetery.

You can see many luxuries inside the house, including fine furniture and china.

The 1914 schoolhouse is an impressive brick building.

Stacks of bunks for students are inside the schoolhouse.

Washington also has several historic trees you can see as you walk around town. These immense trees have withstood time and the elements and are part of the unique history of Washington.

How to get to Historic Washington State Park:

Historic Washington State Park is located at 103 Franklin St, in Washington, Arkansas.

Rush Ghost Town

R*ush* was founded in the late 1880s when zinc carbonate was found. The population of Rush peaked in 1914 to 1917, when the town reached about 5000 people.

At its peak, Rush contained tent homes, houses, stores, offices, a post office, a courthouse, and the Morning Star mill, which opened in 1898.

Mining was abandoned at the end of World War I, and Rush declined shortly afterward.

The buildings you can see today are from the early 1900s, and were abandoned in the 1960s.

Members of the Rush milling crew worked ten hour days, five to six days per week, for 20 to 35 cents per hour.

Walking inside the buildings is discouraged due to the poor preservation and unsafe conditions.

How to get to Rush Ghost Town:

Rush ghost town is located at the end of Marion County Road 6035 off Hwy. 14.

Voices from the past:

"They built a rock furnace, charged it with charcoal, put in their ore, and started the blast. From the opening in the bottom, no silver came, but the prettiest rainbows imaginable floated over the stack of their blast." **Otto Ruhl, Mining and Engineering Journal, 1911.**

"(Bill Taylor) married us right across this showcase he had there with the candy goodies...he had (marriage) papers and they was just a shaking. I really got tickled. I ought to been the one a shaking myself instead of him." **Ware Luffoon, Rush resident.**

"My daddy...was almost killed...in the mines. It caved in and they heard gravel and felt it hitting their hats. They started running, well it did kill one man. It caught him. He almost got out, but he didn't. But the rest of them got out." **Nadine Goodall, Rush storekeeper.**

Arkansas Post

***A**rkansas Post* is located strategically along the Arkansas
River, which became a major transportation route. The post
was intended to be a trading area for New France and the Gulf

of Mexico in the late 1600s. Henri de Tonti acquired the land in 1682, and he established a trading post there four years later. In 1687, survivors of an expedition led by LaSalle stumbled upon Arkansas Post, seeing a large cross, and French-styled buildings. In 1699, Arkansas fort was abandoned, only to be rebuilt again in 1721, this time as a military garrison. The land changed hands from the French to the Spanish in 1763. The fort was moved in 1779 due to flooding, and was renamed Fort Carlos III.

The Bright and Company Trading House was built in 1804 and functioned until 1807. One year after being established, the trading post was doing $25,000 in trade, which was half of the business done at the post. Jacob Bright died suddenly in 1807, Shortly after

Bright's death, the trading post was closed. The site was converted to Montgomery's Tavern by William Montgomery in 1818. It became a meeting place for townspeople and militia. John James Audubon stayed at the tavern in 1820. The tavern closed in 1821.

A trading post was built by the US in 1805, and the population grew to about 500 people by 1810. Arkansas Post was named the capital of Arkansas Territory in 1819. Little Rock became the capital in 1821.

Arkansas Post was a site of conflict during the Civil War, when gunships came up the Arkansas River and fired on the fort in January, 1863. The battering from the gunships destroyed much of the fort and the town, leading to the surrender of the Confederates. They suffered casualties of 60 killed, 80 wounded, and 4971 were imprisoned. The Union Army suffered losses of 134 killed, 898 wounded, and 29 missing. The town never recovered after the Civil War and railroads took over as the main transport and trade.

Six flags have flown over Arkansas Post in its history since 1686. The first was France, when LaSalle claimed the land for France in 1682. Next came Spain in 1763, followed once again by France in 1803. Next came the United States in 1804, followed by the Confederate flag from 1861 to 1863. The stars and stripes once again flew over Arkansas Post beginning in 1863, and continues today.

The Arkansas Post Museum has a fine collection of artifacts from the fort and town. One of my favorite pieces is the Robe of the Three Villages, created around 1740. The three Quapaw villages of Kappa, Tourima, and Osotouy are shown, along with Arkansas Fort in the lower right corner. This is most likely the earliest drawing of Arkansas Post.

There are five historic buildings on the street before you enter the park, including the Refeld-Hinman House, built in 1877, and the Carnes-Bonner Playhouse, built in 1933.

Other buildings include the main house and summer kitchen.

How to get to Arkansas Post:

Arkansas Post is located at 5530 hwy. 165 South, in Gillett, Arkansas.

Voices from the past:

" Being come to a River, that was between us and the Village, and looking over to the further Side, we discover'd a great Cross, and at a small Distance from it, a House, built after the French Fashion. It is hard to express the Joy conceive'd on both Sides; ours was unspeakable, for having at last found, what we had so earnestly desired..." **Henri Joutel, 1687, one of the six surviving members of the La Salle expedition, on sighting Arkansas Post.**

Profiles in history:

Henri de Tonti was born in Paris in 1650 and entered the French army at age 18. He lost his right hand from a grenade explosion. The hand was replaced with a metal extremity, which de Tonti hid with a glove. The Native Americans believed that de Tonti had magical powers, and they called him " Tonti of the Iron Hand." De Tonti established the first trading post at Arkansas Post in 1686, leaving 6 men who were tasked with beginning trade with the local Quapaw Indians.

Interesting fact:

The Arkansas post is the site of the only Revolutionary War battle fought in Arkansas, a skirmish known as Colbert's Raid. On April 17, 1783, British partisans led by James Colbert attacked the Spanish troops at Arkansas Post. The Spanish ultimately repelled Colbert's invaders.

Plum Bayou

***P**lum Bayou Archaeological State Park* is named after a
nearby waterway. The site was originally named the Toltec
Mounds by Gilbert and Mary Knapp, the owners of the site from

1848 to 1905. They believed the mounds were built by the Toltecs from Mexico.

The culture which actually built the mounds lived there from 650 to 1050 AD. There were originally at least 18 mounds at the site, and the mounds were surrounded by a 10-foot tall embankment made of earth. This embankment wall is thought to have been to mark the boundary between the sacred area inside the embankment, and the common area outside.

Only about 50 people lived inside the embankment. These were thought to have been the religious and societal leaders and families of the Plum Bayou people. The Plum Bayou site also contained a central plaza where ceremonies, games, and festivals were held.

Most of the mounds are platform mounds, believed to have been the foundation for a structure or residence built on top of them. One conical shaped mound, known as Mound C, was a burial mound. Through excavations done in the 1960s, human remains were found lying on top of each other, with the mound eventually reaching 12 feet in height.

Excavations also revealed fragments of a conch shell which came from the Gulf of Mexico. The presence of the conch shell indicates the Plum Bayou people traded with tribes living along the Mississippi River.

How to get to Plum Bayou Archaeological State Park:

The Plum Bayou Archaeological State Park is located at 490 Toltec Mounds Road, in Scott, Arkansas.

A Helpful Timeline:

The various periods of occupation in early North America can be confusing. Don't be surprised if you read slightly different dates from other sources, but these are some general guidelines to know about:

The *Paleo-Indian Period, from 10,000 to 8500 BC*, is characterized by hunting and gathering, and small family groups in temporary camps. Artifacts from this period include spears and darts.

The *Archaic Period, from 8500 to 500 BC*, is characterized by some cultivation, and small base settlements. Artifacts from this period include stone, shell, and copper items.

The *Early Woodland Period, from 500 BC to 1 AD*, is characterized by permanent villages, organization under a tribal or religious leader, and elite burials in mounds. Artifacts from this period include the addition of clay pottery.

The *Middle Woodland Period, from 1 AD to 400 AD*, is characterized by the introduction of maize, long-distance trade, and elite burials with precious objects. Burial mounds, platform mounds, and earthworks were built.

The *Late Woodland Period, from 400 AD to 800 AD*, is characterized by cultivated seed plants, large permanent villages, and use of the bow and arrow.

The *Early Mississippian Period, from 800 AD to 1300 AD*, is characterized by cultivation of corn, beans, and squash, with permanent villages and farming settlements. Temples and houses of leaders were built on mounds in major villages. Pottery and artistic forms were developed.

The *Late Mississippian Period, from 1300 AD to 1700 AD*, is characterized by towns enclosed in stockade walls, increased power among chiefs and religious leaders. Increased and more elaborate artistic representations on pottery, shells, and wood were also more common.

Little Rock

L*ittle Rock* is a lovely major city. One of the most charming sites to see is ***The Old Mill***. Parts of the current old mill are replicated from the original structure used by pioneers in the 1800s.

The first floor of the current building is original, dating from 1828.

The faux wood design of the mill was created by Dionicio Rodriguez, a well-known Mexican sculptor.

The Old Mill was featured in the opening credits of Gone with the Wind, filmed in 1938.

How to get to the Old Mill:

The Old Mill is located at 3800 Lakeshore Dr. in Little Rock.

Interesting fact:

In the summer of 1952, a massive alligator was captured in Arkansas in a farmer's pasture. The amazing reptile measured over 13 feet and weighed over 500 pounds. The alligator, known as "Big Arky" lived in the Little Rock Zoo for 18 years. Big Arky died in 1970 and his remains live on, displayed at the Arkansas State University Museum in Jonesboro.

Jacksonport State Park

*J*acksonport State Park preserves the site of Jacksonport, laid out in 1834. It became an important river town and steamboat port.

The Civil War saw the installation of both the Union and Confederate armies. Five generals used Jacksonport for their headquarters. In 1865, Confederate General Jeff Thompson surrendered over 5000 troops to Union Lt. Colonel C.W. Davis.

Today you can see the courthouse, built from 1869 to 1872. The ornate balconies were once used for political speeches.

Newport became the county seat in 1892, so the courthouse was used as a school, cotton gin, and a poor house. Jacksonport was bypassed by the railroad in the 1870s.

How to get to Jacksonport State Park:

Jacksonport State Park is located at 111 Avenue Street, in Newport.

Voices from the past:

"The South went to war on account of slavery...because slavery would not be secure under Lincoln...I am not ashamed of having fought on the side of slavery. A soldier fights for his country, right or wrong. He is not responsible for the political merits of the course he fights in...The South was my country." **John Mosby, Confederate partisan leader.**

"Once let the black man get upon his person the brass letters, U-S, let him get an eagle on his button, and a musket on his shoulder and bullets in his pockets, and there is no power on earth which can deny that he has earned the right to citizenship in the United States." **Frederick Douglass**

Hampson

The ***Hampson Archaeological Museum*** contains a collection from the Nodena culture, who lived in the area from 1400 to 1650 AD.

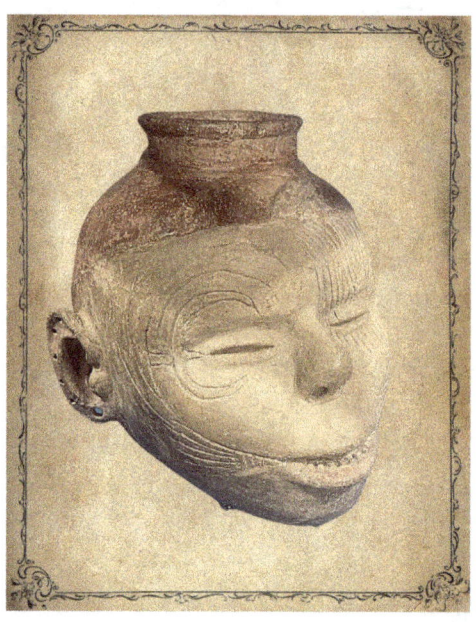

One of the most fascinating artifacts in the collection is this head pot. The closed eyes, slightly open lips, and flipped birdman figure covering the left eye, may indicate this is an effigy of someone who has died.

Red and white pottery are indicative of the Nodena culture. This type of pottery was reserved for ceremonies.

Dr. James Hampson was an amateur archaeologist who did extensive excavation and research on the site. There are no mounds on the site, because they have been destroyed by farming.

How to get to Hampson:

Hampson Archaeological Museum State Park is located at 33 Park Avenue, in Wilson, Arkansas.

A word about Chunkey:

The game of chunkey, also spelled chungke, was a common entertainment for many cultures, including the Nodena. The game was played by two men, one of whom rolled a stone disk, known as a Chunkey stone. He and his opponent threw sticks, known as Tchung-kees, to where they thought the stone would stop rolling. The one closest to the stone earned points. Chunkey stones have been found in many sites in the Eastern United States, often as a grave good.

Parkin

***P**arkin* was established during the late Mississippian period, and is believed to be the Native American village of Casqui. The bridge in the photo crosses a defensive ditch and palisade area, which circled the village, protecting it from raiding Indian groups. The village flourished from 1350 to 1650 AD.

Hernando de Soto visited the site in 1541. De Soto is said to have erected a large cross at Parkin. A large charred post was excavated at the summit of the temple mound in 1966. These fragments are from a bald cypress tree which was cut between 1515 and 1663. It's an intriguing thought that this could be part of the cross, but we do not know for sure.

The De Soto expedition wrote about warfare and raiding between the groups of indigenous people at or near Parkin. Small farmsteads gave way to everyone living in a fortified village, like Parkin. The Parkin site itself is believed to have been the ceremonial center for the villages surrounding it.

The Parkin site consists of a temple mound, ditch, a village area within the ditch, and a borrow pit outside the ditch. The mound is a flat-topped pyramidal mound, which formed the foundation of a temple or chief's house.

The museum at Parkin contains a fine collection of artifacts. One of the most beautiful is this gorget, or medallion, in the shape of a turtle, and made from a turtle shell.

Artifacts from Parkin include two head pots, projectile points, scrapers, bone awls, needles, and fishhooks. The head pots may represent trophy heads of captives.

Chevron glass beads and a brass bell were also found. These two items were common gifts given by the Spanish. The small bells are known as Clarksdale Bells and were used in falconry. This bell was found around the neck of a child buried hundreds of years ago.

There is a spur trail at Parkin that leads to the Northern Ohio School, built around 1910. The school operated for 38 years to teach children of the Coldren plantation and the Northern Ohio Cooperage and Lumber Company. This school closed in 1948.

How to get to Parkin:

The Parkin Archaeological State Park is located at 60 hwy. 184 N. in Parkin, Arkansas.

Voices from the past:

"For two days the governor (de Soto) marched through the land of Casqui before arriving at the town where the cacique was, and most of the way continually through land of open field, very well peopled with large towns, two or three of which were to be seen from one town..." **Account by a Gentleman from Elvas.**

"In my opinion, in a (Chief) of such discretion as Casqui, it would have seemed well to baptize him and make him and his people Christians; and it would have been better to stay there, than to go forward to what this history will relate." **Account by Rodrigo Rangel.**

A word about cultures, traditions, and periods:

A *culture* is a specific social group with a unique way of life. An example is the Adena culture, identified by conical burial mounds, copper artifacts, and specific shapes of beads and pipes.

A *tradition*, is a broadly identified way of life, in use by different cultures at different time periods.The Woodland Tradition can be identified across many cultures in many geographic locations. Woodland tradition is identified by the beginning of agriculture, pottery making, and the establishment of permanent villages.

A *period*, is a specified span of time during which one tradition is dominant. The Woodland Tradition has several periods including the burial mound period of 1000 BC to 700 AD. A period is a method of measuring time.

Powhatan Historic State Park

*P*owhatan Historic State Park is named after Pocahontas's father, Chief Powhatan. The town of Powhatan was incorporated in 1853, after the Osage Indians were relocated in 1817. The park has six historic buildings in their original locations.

The immense Courthouse, built in 1888, sits on a hill above the townsite. The current courthouse was erected on the original courthouse grounds.

The original courthouse was built in 1873. The land was purchased for $800, and the courthouse construction cost was $16,723.38.

The courthouse contains a nice museum, full of artifacts and history from the town.

The jail was built of native limestone and was constructed before the courthouse. It was home to prisoners for 57 years, but was eventually closed in the 1920s.

Prisoners convicted of capital crimes were executed by being hung from a nearby tree.

There is a log cabin among the collection of structures near the courthouse. It's made of hand-hewn logs, and was built in the mid 19th century. It's known as the Ficklin-Imogen Cabin. The cabin has a separate kitchen building, to reduce the risk of fire destroying the main house.

The brick commercial building dates to 1887, 12 years after telephone was invented. The building became Lawrence County's first telephone exchange. The commercial building was also a drug store, law office, post office, general store, and a residence.

The Laurel was the first steamboat to arrive in Powhatan in 1829. In 1837, John Ficklin, the founder of Powhatan, established a ferry on the Black River. Powhatan declined when the Frisco Railroad bypassed the town.

How to get to Powhatan State Park:

Powhatan State Park is located at 4414 AR-25, in Lawrence County, Arkansas.

Voices from the past:

"The average farmer's wife is one of the most patient and over-worked women of the time." **The American Farmer, 1884.**

A word about the Pearl Rush:

The Black River in Arkansas is home to freshwater mussels. In 1897, a large pearl was found in a mussel, igniting a rush to discover more pearls. Many camps grew along the the Black River, filled with pearl prospectors. Buttons made out of the mussel shells became so popular that mussel harvesting was kept alive for years.

Favorite Places to Camp

*C*ane Creek State Park is in the quaint town of Star City, Arkansas. It's wooded, spacious, and beautiful. There are 29 campsites with electric and water hookups, showers, and a dump station onsite. The park is located at 50 State Park Road, Star City, AR. For reservations, please visit ***ArkansasStateParks.com***

Lake Ouachita State Park is lovely, and is named after the largest lake in Arkansas. It boasts spectacular natural beauty, 93 campsites (58 Class AAA, 23 Class D, and 12 walk-in tent sites), some right on the water. There are also 8 fully-equipped cabins with kitchens. For reservations, please visit ***ArkansasStatePar ks.com***

Jacksonport State Park is yet another spectacular state park in Arkansas. This state park has 20 Class A campsites (50 amp service), a swimming beach, pavilion, picnic sites, a playground, and the half-mile Tunstall Riverwalk. For reservations, please visit *ArkansasStateParks.com*

Random Thoughts

What History Means to Me

First, let me start by sharing with you my opinion of what history isn't. History is not a collection of random dates, names, and places for you to memorize. History is not a dry and uninteresting class you have to pass to graduate.

I believe history is a tangible thing. You can actually *feel* history in the places you go, and the sights you see. I remember walking up to the Acropolis in Athens. I looked down at the well-worn marble steps and wondered about how many ancient philosophers had climbed these very steps, thousands of years ago.

You don't have to go far away to experience the *feeling* of history. If you are lucky enough to live in an old house, you may experience history in your own surroundings. You might say to yourself, *"If only these walls could talk."*

During my travels across the United States, I *felt* history in many, many places. If you travel across the country like I did, you will *feel* the wonderful history of our beautiful country for yourself, and you will never be the same. You will discover what it means to be an American.

Why I travel, and why you should too:

I decided to travel across the country by car because I wanted to rediscover America. When I first set out to explore the history of our country, I wanted to find out why America is the greatest country on earth, and what it means to be an American.

The politics of these United States can be frightening and polarizing. I prefer to focus on what unites us, not what divides us. What unites us is we all live in a spectacularly beautiful country, with warm, wonderful people.

I began my journey five years ago, starting out in my Honda CRV. I soon realized I loved the lifestyle, so now I travel in a small RV. From my small RV, I look out on a country with a unique and colorful, multicultural tapestry, unlike any other country on earth.

I have a degree in Archaeology, and a passion for all things archaeological. I love history, with a side love of paleontology. It is these three passions that I set my trip agenda around. I set out to discover the archaeological sites, history, and paleontological world of our country.

As I travel and write my books, I get asked all the time, especially by women, "What is it like to travel by yourself? Aren't you scared?" The truth is, I believe everyone should do what I did. It's a wonderful way to discover our country, and to rediscover yourself. The truth is, I'm scared not to travel. Traveling allows you to get to know yourself, in ways not possible when sitting on the couch watching TV.

We tend to spend a lot of our lives tuning out the world and our place within it. When you travel, you are quite literally forced to deal with your own thoughts, emotions, and feelings. You can discover yourself while traveling. You can come to understand what makes you who you are, and how you can perhaps become a better person. Above all, traveling gives you mental clarity to figure out how to live with intent. It's a way to guide your life, not just wait for things to happen.

Travel Tips & Stuff

What You Need to Know

How to get started:

P lanning your trip should be one of the most exciting things about it. You want to be spontaneous, but it is also very wise to plan your route, so you can take full advantage of all the time and miles you will invest.

- First, decide your passions. If you love airplanes, trains, or old vehicles, plan your trip around that. If you love gardens or architecture, seek that out as the focus of your trip.

- Next, read and research areas of the country that will let you enjoy what you are interested in.

- Make a list by state and city or town, of what you want to see.

- Take your handy road atlas and locate the areas on the pages.

- Make a tentative route plan, so you have an idea of where you are going.

Travel tip: Avoid trying to plan your trip down to a schedule of days, hours, or minutes. On a road trip, it will be virtually impossible to know where you will be on any given day. If you adhere to a schedule, you are more likely to stress out, and less likely to actually enjoy yourself, which is the whole point.

What you need:

You need to bring along a sense of adventure and a curious mind. You need to ditch the idea of always being on a schedule, and live a little more spontaneously to thoroughly enjoy yourself. Things will happen as you travel, both good things and bad things, and you need to prepare your mind and your soul for day-to-day changes.

So much of our lives are planned out. Between growing up, going to school, finding a career, marriage, kids, or whatever, people have lost much of the ability to be spontaneous. But you must take spontaneity on the trip with you, because you may make detours along the way to see something really spectacular.

So, for the practical stuff you need:

A great vehicle-I am now five years into the trip and have swapped out my Honda CRV for a small RV, just under 20 feet. I go small because I see humongous RVs on the road, towing a car behind, and all I can think of is, they can't go just anywhere. They are too big. Bad gas mileage, cumbersome to drive, slow, and not agile like my small RV. So, I encourage you, if you want to go car or RV camping and be able to go on remote dirt roads, get an agile vehicle, and small RVs are great.

Travel tip: Don't be afraid to do some modifications to your vehicle. I have made many alterations to my RV, including changing the plumbing, which used to be a mere 4 inches off of the ground, so I would break it all the time. It's now encased in my outside storage compartment. I am also a minimalist, so I have jettisoned anything I won't use or don't love. Don't be afraid to get rid of unnecessary stuff.

An awesome camera that you know inside and out. I use a Nikon and it takes wonderful pictures. Don't skimp on a camera, and don't think a cellphone camera is all you need, because you want the best for your beautiful photos.

Window shades-the best ones are magnetic so you just place them against your windows and they cling to them, obscuring the view inside your car. I also have magnetic window screens, so I can leave my windows down with no bugs!

Battery operated fans and lights-these are important, so you don't have to rely on your house batteries for light and cooling options.

Portable air compressor-this little gem plugs into your cigarette lighter and will inflate your tires if you have a flat. Make sure the air compressor can reach to all of your tires, including your rear tires.

Portable battery charger and power bank-mine comes with battery cables and the power bank, yet once inside the case, it is small enough to put in your glove compartment. This little item, unfortunately, I have had to use, and it saved me.

Portable generator-I have two gas powered generators on the back of my RV, which are hooked together with a coupling unit. I have an interior generator, but after much expense and multiple repairs, it still doesn't work. Now I have generators which will run everything, including AC, and I can maintain them myself.

All season clothing-you never know what different states will bring for weather, so take hot weather and cold weather clothes, and a fair amount of shoes appropriate for hiking, or walking, sandals, and slippers, which are nice at night. Also take along a pair of cheap rubber flip-flops to wear in the public showers you might go into.

Your own pillows-I like my own pillows, so I don't wake up with neck cramps, especially after sleeping in the car.

Sleeping bag and cozy blankets-you want to stay warm and layering is everything.

Warm hat, warm socks, and fuzzy jammies to keep you warm for cold nights sleeping in the car.

A great road atlas, and great guidebooks-get one that's easy to read, with great pictures. For a road atlas, just get one that is easy to read.

A word about photography:

Along with a great camera, you need to have a great eye. This is easier than it sounds once you have worked with your camera and are comfortable taking pictures with it. I am not a professional photographer, but I like my pictures and other people do too.

These are my tips for taking great pictures:

- Experiment with taking both horizontal and vertical shots.

- Don't always put the subject of the photo in the middle of the photograph.

- This one is important: pay attention to the foreground, and if possible, have something, a plant or whatever, in the foreground to help give the photo dimension and depth.

- This one is important too: turn around often to see the view you just came from. I do this quite often and some of my best pictures have resulted from when I turned around and took the shot.

You can also take a mental photo. Place an image in your mind that you can call upon later. Use all of your senses to see, hear, smell, and maybe even to taste, what is around you. You have the means to fully experience your surroundings, and that is very important to a traveler. When you take a mental photo, be sure to jot down quick little details about what you saw, heard, smelled, or tasted, so you can jog your memory later.

And last, but not least...don't be posing in front of everything, everywhere, to show that you actually went somewhere. Most people want to see themselves in your photo and be mentally transported there, but they can't if you are there already.⧄

To camp or not to camp:

Car or RV camping is great. I prefer it to sleeping on the cold, hard ground in a tent. I can lock the doors, put my window shades up and be cozy for the night.

Some people camp in a Walmart parking lot and feel safe. I do not. I believe that if you are in a busy area, you are more likely to be confronted by a nut job who may bother you. Nothing against Walmart, and many Walmart stores don't allow overnight parking. I don't go for rest areas either because they have a track record of incidents happening to people in rest areas, especially women travelers.

I have come to love casino parking lots. I enjoy gambling, so for a little money, many casinos will provide overnight stays if you gamble a little inside the casino. I also do a lot of boondocking, because it's free, and I believe you are safer parked out in the middle of nowhere in the dark.

I also enjoy camping in state or national campgrounds, wildlife sanctuaries, and fairgrounds.

A word about safety:

When you are a woman traveling alone, it's critical to keep a low profile. Don't tell people you are traveling alone, where you are staying, or any other personal information.

I don't go to bars or get drunk. I'm not preaching but you are on your own, in a city or town you've never been to, and you don't know anyone, so it's not the time to lose control of what you are doing. When you are in control, you are better able to decide which people you want to get to know better.

Travel tip: If you feel vulnerable traveling alone, that's OK. Vulnerability is part of passion, and traveling is a passionate thing to do. You can put one of those family stickers on your vehicle to indicate to others that you are not traveling alone, which can help you feel more secure.

Maintain your connections:

When you are traveling alone, there is a definite sense of discon-nection. It feels almost like you are the only one in the world, traveling through space and time. That's why it's critical to keep your connections to loved ones active.

Be on Facebook while you are traveling. You may not have internet a lot of the time, or the internet will be poor. Consider paying to have your phone be a hotspot. It's a little bit of money per month, but it's worth it and has saved me from being without internet. I love the convenience of it, and you will too.

Plan your journey around visiting family members or friends you haven't seen for a long time, or people that are good friends. When you see people you know, it will ground you, so you can continue traveling.

Check in by phone with loved ones. They worry about you, and it's good for both of you to stay connected no matter where you are.

Consider traveling with a pet. I now travel with my 12 year-old sheltie Rosie, after losing my beloved sheltie, Sadie. Rosie is a wonderful companion. She is also an excellent watchdog, and barks her head off at other dogs and people.

Travel tip: One of the easiest and best ways I stay connected while traveling is to offer to take a photo for someone I don't know. Many couples, families, or singles would love to have more pictures of themselves traveling. It's an easy and quick way to have a connection with a fellow traveler, and it's good manners too.

Practical matters:

You need to have an address to send your mail to. Keep in touch with whomever is nice enough to do this for you.

You will also need to come back occasionally to register your car, vote, go to doctor visits, and take care of any other business. You can't leave it all behind, as tempting as that may be.

Bad things that happened:

I have had a few problems, mostly associated with my RV. I bought an older model, vintage 1999, and I have had to do a few repairs.

My worst experience came when I took my rig in to a shop in Spokane, Washington (who shall remain nameless.) All I needed was an oil change. I got the oil change and was about an hour south of town on a Friday at 4:30, when my engine blew.

I was in the middle of the eastern Washington prairie, many miles from the nearest town. All I could do was watch my oil drain out onto the Interstate. I can't help but think it was associated with my oil change, but I couldn't prove it. The moral of this story is: DON'T LET JUST ANYONE WORK ON YOUR VEHICLE.

Good things that happened:

I have met many great people on my travels, from all walks of life. I have also learned not to judge people. I have met numerous homeless people who are often just wanting a kind word, and not to be treated like dirt.

People have mistaken me for a homeless person, and I too, have been treated like dirt. When I can, I try to help people and be kind to them. Most of the time, they smile and reciprocate. You will always meet people who are unkind, but they are just as likely to be driving a huge expensive rig, or to be homeless.

We are all Americans, and we are all part of the human race. When you meet people across the country, you realize just how important it is to get to know your fellow citizens, and learn more about how they view the world and our country.

I have to give a special shout-out to the many dedicated people, often volunteers, who staff our state and national parks and monuments. They work tirelessly to ensure the health of our natural resources, and help travelers enjoy their visit. The same is true of the many people who staff the museums in small towns and large cities. They enjoy history, like I do, and it shows in their smiles.

Along with wonderful people, I have seen an America that is spectacularly beautiful, with open prairies, majestic mountains, and crystal clear rivers. I have seen a small fraction of the history of our country. I have seen the memorials to the brave people who shaped our country. I have fallen in love with America in a way that was not possible sitting in my living room. People ask me, "would I do it again?" The answer comes easily, "Yes, in a heartbeat."

Bibliography

Arkansas Post, National Park Service, 2022

Arkansas Post Museum, Arkansas Department of Parks & Tourism, 2015

Arkansas State Parks Guide, Arkansas Department of Parks, Heritage and Tourism

Brown, Alan, *Ghosts of the South*, The History Press, 2021

Cane Creek State Park brochure, Arkansas State Parks

Coleman, Roger, *The Arkansas Post Story*, Eastern National, 2023

Fort Smith, National Park Service, 2023

Historic Washington State Park Self-Guided Walking Tour

Jacksonport State Park, Arkansas Department of Parks & Tourism 2022

Morse, Phyllis, *Parkin Arkansas Archeological Survey Research Series No. 13*, Fayetteville, AR. 2023

Pea Ridge National Military Park, National Park Service, 2022

Plum Bayou Mounds Archaeological State Park brochure, Arkansas Department of Parks, Heritage, & Tourism

Plum Bayou Mounds Archaeological State Park Knapp Trail Guide, Arkansas State Parks

Powhatan Historic State Park, Arkansas Department of Parks & Tourism 2012

Prairie Grove Battlefield State Park, Arkansas Department of Parks & Tourism, 2014

Prairie Grove Battlefield Trail, Arkansas Department of Parks & Tourism, 2011

Self-Guided Driving Tour of the Prairie Grove Battlefield, Arkansas Department of Parks & Tourism, 2011

Shiloh Museum brochure

Silverberg, Robert, *The Mound Builders*, Ohio University Press, 1970

Steed, Bud, *Haunted Northwest Arkansas*, The History Press, 2017

Underwood, Edward L. and Karen J. *Forgotten Tales of Arkansas*, The History Press, 2012

Index

Referenced by Sections

B

C

D

E

F

M

MacArthur, Douglas-see Famous People from Arkansas

McCullough, General Ben-see Pea Ridge National Military Park

Mississippian Period-see Parkin

Montgomery's Tavern-see Arkansas Post

Montgomery, William-see Arkansas Post

Morning Star Mill-see Rush

Mosby, John-see Jacksonport State Park

N

New France-see Arkansas Post

Nodena Culture-see Hampson

Northern Ohio Cooperage and Lumber Company-see Parkin

Northern Ohio School-see Parkin

O

Old Mill-see Little Rock

Osage Indians-see Powhatan

Overland Stage-see Pea Ridge National Military Park

Ozark Mountains-see The Shiloh Museum,

T

The American Farmer-see Powhatan

Thompson, General Jeff-see Jacksonport

Thornton, Billy Bob-see Dreams of Arkansas, Famous People from Arkansas

Toltec Mounds-see Plum Bayou

Trail of Tears-see Pea Ridge National Military Park

U

U.S. Mexican War-see Fort Smith

V

Van Dorn, General Earl-see Pea Ridge National Military Park, Prairie Grove

Voices from the past-see Pea Ridge National Military Park, Prairie Grove, Fort Smith, Rush, Arkansas Post, Jacksonport State Park, Parkin, Powhatan

W

Walton, Sam-see Famous People from Arkansas

Washington, George-see Historic Washington

About the Author

Julie Bettendorf is a world traveler with a degree in archaeology and a background in history. She has traveled extensively throughout Egypt, Central America, South America, Europe, and the United Kingdom, visiting archaeological and historical sites all along the way.

Currently, Julie is traveling around the US visiting ghost towns, ancient rock art sites, and archaeological wonders as part of research for her ongoing historical travel series entitled ***Wandering Woman***. Wandering Woman is a set of state-by-state guides, full of photographs, historical anecdotes, and unique tips to help other women travel and explore solo across the US by car or RV. Julie enjoys writing freelance blogs, traveling frequently with her two adult children, and hiking outdoors with her faithful dog companion Rosie.

Also By Julie Bettendorf

Wandering Woman: Arkansas i**s** the most recent book in the ***Wandering Woman Travel Series*****.** The additional books ***Wandering Woman: Montana, Colorado, Nevada, Utah, Idaho, Oregon, Washington, Arizona, New Mexico, Wyoming, Kansas, Nebraska, South Dakota, North Dakota, Northern California***, ***Southern California, and Oklahoma*** are available in ebook and paperback.

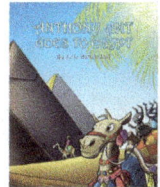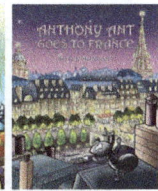

Julie has published two children's books in an ongoing, beautifully illustrated travel series entitled ***Anthony Ant Goes to France*** and ***Anthony Ant Goes to Egypt***.

She has also published a work of historical fiction entitled ***Luxor: Book of Past Lives*** which has recently been released as an audiobook, read by renowned narrator Barry Shannon.